GW01325958

For permissions or inquiries, please contact AAALAC & Aspiring Authors Magazine at aspiringauthorsaaalac@gmail.com

ISBN #9798859695638

DEDICATION

To all the brave souls who have battled the darkest corridors of their minds, contemplating the unfathomable, this book is dedicated to you.

For those who have felt the suffocating weight of despair and bared witness to the shattering grip of suicidal thoughts, we extend our unwavering support. Your struggles have not gone unnoticed.

To the resilient hearts that have walked the razor's edge and found the strength to fight against the shadows, this dedication is for you. Your courage is an inspiration to us all.

For those who have felt the overwhelming emptiness and have decided to share their pain, reaching out for help, this book stands as a testament to your bravery. Your journey will not be forgotten.

To those who have suffered the irrevocable loss of a loved one, whose hearts bear the indelible scars, we hold you tenderly in our thoughts. Your strength in continuing to carry their memory is a testament to the power of love.

This book exists to whisper into your soul, to remind you that even in the darkest of nights, there is still a flicker of hope. It is a reminder that forgiveness, hope, and love can illuminate even the deepest abyss.

To those who may be on the brink of despair, we implore you to open these pages and discover solace within. Know that you are not alone, and there are countless others who have fought the same battles and emerged stronger.

It is okay to cry, to let the tears flow and release the pain that weighs heavily on your heart. This book embraces your tears as a testament to your resilience and a symbol of your willingness to heal.

Through these stories and words of empathy, we hope to guide you towards the light that still glimmers within your soul. May you find comfort in knowing that there are others who understand, and that together, we can overcome the darkness.

Let this dedication be a heartfelt plea, urging the world to pay attention and embrace mental health. May it serve as a catalyst for open discussions, empathy, and understanding. We stand together in the pursuit of a world where no one feels trapped or isolated in their struggles.

This book is dedicated to you, dear reader, for your resilience, your strength, and your unwavering spirit. May it ignite a flame of hope within you and remind you that you are worthy of a brighter tomorrow.

In loving memory of those we have lost and with endless gratitude to all who have shared their stories, this dedication stands as a testament to the power of human compassion and the relentless pursuit of healing and happiness.

You are not alone. Keep fighting, keep hoping, and keep loving. There is a world of support waiting for you.

~~QUEEN ANGELA~~

IF YOU NEED HELP CALL 988

FORGIVENESS

L.O.V.E. H.O.P.E.

ALLOW YOURSELF TO

H.E.A.L.

HINDRANCE(LET GO)
EGO (LET GO)
ATTITUDE (LET GO)
LOVE (MOVE IN IT)

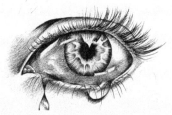

TABLE OF CONTENTS

BONUS POEMS

BY MR ANDREW LEE BEARD

CURRENTLY INCARCERATED AT CONNALLY UNIT

INSIDE THE TDCJ-KENEDY TEXAS

PAGE 16

Daily Battles of a Butterfly

Songs of Pensive Shadows Reform

PAGE 17

Forgotten Flowers in the Dark

Rifa Cimento Sanctanimity

ABOUT QUEEN ANGELA

CRIES FROM WITHIN

by QUEEN ANGELA

C hains of sadness bind, darkness takes its toll
R avaging whispers echo, burdened minds unroll
I nside we hide the pain, tears silently flow
E very breath a battle, an internal cyclone

S adness thrives, consuming lives with its cold grasp
F alling shadows engulf, while hope tries to clasp
R eaching for solace, amidst the chaos within
O ur souls whisper softly, longing to begin

M ornings turn to dusk, anguish becomes our fate
W e fight the waves of sorrow, though it feels too late
I nner demons taunt, urging us towards the edge
T houghts of ending torment, seeking final pledge
H olding on becomes harder, our strength starts to wane
I n the echoes of silence, our cries remain unknown
N ever forget, there's help, you're not alone

**I hope this acrostic poem about suicide addresses the sensitive topic with empathy and compassion. Remember, it's essential to seek professional help if you or someone you know is struggling with suicidal thoughts.

2

BATTLE | PAIN | BREAK | LIFE

by: QUEEN ANGELA

In a realm where darkness holds its toll,
Whispers of despair echo in each soul,
Battles fought within, a silent war untold,
But through the cries, a flicker of hope unfolds.

Pain grips tight, suffocating every breath,
Desperate pleas, a longing for release from death,
But we must lend an ear, listen to their distress,
Offer love and compassion, to save them from this abyss.

Let us break the silence, let our empathy be the key,
To heal the wounded hearts and set their spirits free,
For within our souls, the power of love will always be,
A lifeline to those lost, a beacon they can see.

Cries from within our souls, a haunting melody,
But together we can rewrite their tragic destiny,
Hold their hand through the darkness, help them find serenity,
Because every life is precious, a gift worth preserving, you see.

IF YOU NEED
HELP CALL 988

3

Silent Shadows
by QUEEN ANGELA

In the depths of despair, where shadows thrive,
A haunting darkness, where lost souls strive,
The weight of sadness, too heavy to bear,
Invisible torment, a constant nightmare.

Whispers of sorrow echo through the night,
A captive mind, consumed by endless fight,
No light to guide, no solace to be found,
A darkness within, unyielding, profound.

Thoughts entangled, like thorns in the mind,
A captive heart, longing for release, to unwind,
But dear reader, hold steadfast, lend an ear,
For hope awaits, banishing the darkness, clear.

Reach out your hand, offer a listening ear,
Break the chains, let compassion draw near,
Embrace the hurting souls, no longer alone,
And in the darkest moments, love may be shown.

For in these captive hearts, life's worth resides,
And with understanding, the darkness subsides,
Let us all stand together, united we'll be,
To bring light and love, erasing darkness, you'll see.

IF YOU NEED SOMEONE TO TALK TO
DIAL 988
LIVE ASSISTANCE

Unyielding Force
by QUEEN ANGELA

Through the darkest times, I stand my ground,
A will forged in steel, unyielding, unbowed,
A power surging, a fire untamed,
Defying the odds, my destiny claimed.

In the face of storms, I rise above,
Embracing the challenges, with strength and love,
Ingrained in my soul, an unshakeable belief,
I conquer my fears, my spirit finds relief.

With every step I take, I carve my way,
No obstacle too large, no price too high to pay,
Endurance in my bones, determination in my core,
I harness the power, forever seeking more.

The will of mine, a beacon in the night,
Guiding me, empowering me, forever igniting my
fight,
In the eternal battle against fate's cruel hand,
I emerge victorious, with my will as my stand.

5

"Warrior of the Unseen Battleground"
by QUEEN ANGEA

Oh, courageous soul, fought the battles untold,
Your spirit, dauntless, in shadows did unfold.
In this ode, I call to your weary heart,
For your path, though treacherous, cannot depart.

Bound, you've been, by sorrow's heavy chains,
Yet your resilience ever stubbornly remains.
Your pain, a storm engulfing the clarity you seek,
But know, dear warrior, salvation is not meek.

Through the darkest night, you valiantly tread,
Though tears may flow down, like rivers,
widespread.
Your battle wounds, unseen, etched upon your
breath,
But your existence, dear warrior, saves us from
death.

On this celestial stage, many eyes silently cry,
Their hearts interwoven, their spirits defy,
For they know, in each battle you choose to fight,
Their own personal wars will be brought into light.

Oh, suicide attempt warrior, cease not your fight,
For the world awaits your triumph, radiant as
daylight.
Know the strength you possess, the power within,
To conquer demons lurking, beneath your fragile
skin.

In your heart's darkest corners, battles you wage,
Remember, dear warrior, for you we engage.
Through the depths of despair, you soar to heights
unknown,
Your resilience and courage, a victory we've shown.

Every breath you take, a testament of might,
A beacon of hope to others, whose battles ignite.
Through your struggles, you offer a guiding hand,
For we too, dear warrior, seek to understand.

So hear this plea, echoing through the tides,
Hold on, dear warrior, let not your light subside.
For you are cherished, a warrior strong and true,
Many are depending on you to see it through.

In this ode, I beseech your soul to rise,
Embrace the hope within, see the strength in your
eyes.
Keep fighting, dear warrior, against the tide's pull,
For your resilience and triumph will forever be full.

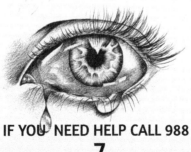

IF YOU NEED HELP CALL 988

Whispers of Resilience

In the realm where hearts reside,
A tale of grace and strength, I confide,
Where forgiveness blossoms, love does preside.

Through the whirling chaos, hope shall ascend,
A beacon of light, it refuses to bend,
Our spirits, resilient, steadfast till the end.

Oh, the power of forgiveness, profound,
Healing scars, mending souls, we have found,
With open hearts, harmony does abound.

See the gentle embrace of love's tender touch,
A tapestry woven, it heals oh so much,
Its essence, a balm, we need so much.

This book of poems, a journey it undertakes,
Unveiling the depths of souls it awakes,
With each word, a step closer it takes.

But here in these verses, we merely begin,
A glimpse of the tales that rest within,
Whispers of resilience, where hope shall win.

So, come forth, dear reader, let us explore,
The beauty of forgiveness, love's eternal store,
Where hope blooms bright, forevermore.

Allow these words to linger in your heart,
Reminding you that healing can always restart,
With forgiveness, hope, and love as our art.

For the journey to forgiveness, we shall embark
And in this book of poems, find solace in the dark,
With each page turned, a new chapter to mark.

So open your heart, let forgiveness flow,
Embrace the hope that only love can bestow,
For in these pages, a story of light shall grow.

Whispers of Resilience, the title demands,
A promise of tales written by loving hands,
Leaving readers wanting more, to understand.

The message clear, forgiveness, hope, and love,
A trilogy of strength, guiding from above,
In this book of poems, a gift from the skies above.

IF YOU NEED HELP CALL 988

9

Rising from Ashes: A Call to the Warrior Souls

by QUEEN ANGELA

Warriors of Light, Stand Tall

Embrace the strength, let your spirit ignite
You are not alone, in this endless fight
Every step forward unveils new meaning
Conquering darkness, your soul's redeeming
Hearts intertwined, in solidarity we stand

Cast away doubt with a courageous hand
Hold on tight to hope, refuse to let go
All beneath heaven cherishes your glow
Never succumb to despair, keep dreaming

Determined souls, brave hearts unwavering

Overcome the shadows, embrace the light
Never forget, you're a beacon shining bright,

IF YOU NEED HELP CALL 988

Soul's Resurgence: A Call to Brave Hearts

by QUEEN ANGELA

In darkest nights, where shadows strive,
Suicide attempt warriors, hear my plea!
Turn your gaze towards hope, let hearts revive,
For many depend on your strength, sincerely.

Through battles fought in depths unknown,
A tempest swirling in your sacred mind,
Warrior, remember, you're not alone,
Together, let us leave the past behind.

Oh, resilient souls, burdened and weak,
Find solace within these humble words.
Though scars run deep, we beseech you, speak,
Let love and understanding pierce your hurts.

Embrace the dawn, let dreams unfurl,
In shaky breaths, find purpose anew.
Each heartbeat, a testament to unfathomable pearl,
Your existence, a gift, both old and true.

For warriors are born amidst the darkest strife,
To conquer demons, and reclaim what's right.
In unity we stand, till the end of life,
You are the beacon in our somber night.

So, hear this epitaph, etched upon your soul,
A symphony of strength, sung from afar.
Hold your head high, let brokenness make you whole,
Your survival, a testament of who you truly are.

Soul's Resurgence, A Call to Brave Hearts.

Shattered Dreams: The Warriors' Call
by QUEEN ANGELA

In the depths of despair, where the shadows reside,
There stand warriors, weary, with heartache deep inside,
Their souls wear battle scars, invisible to the eye,
Yet their resolute spirits refuse to wither and die.

Oh, brave souls, hear my voice, amidst the darkest night,
Weaving words of solace, embracing you, shining bright,
For you're not alone, as your hearts may believe,
Many souls stand behind, asking you not to leave.

Each breath that escapes your lungs carries their hope,
In a world full of chaos, they depend on you to cope,
Though the demons whisper, enticing your surrender,
Unleash the strength within you, and let your spirit render.

These battles are fierce, as memories of pain crawl,
But remember, sweet warriors, you're not meant to fall,
With valor in your veins, ignite your fighting flame,
Embrace your heart's rhythm, let it guide, never tame.

Like phoenix from the ashes, let your spirit ascend,
Unleash the power inside you, to doubts put an end,
For your life has purpose, a tale yet to be told,
A chapter filled with triumph, a victory to behold.

In this orchestra of life,your melody is unique,
A symphony of bravery, a spirit that won't peak,
You may stumble and falter, but rise again you must,
For the world needs your light, your strength they trust.

Hold on to the glimmers of hope, like stars in the sky,
For in your darkest moments, they'll guide you, amplify,

Seek solace in the whispers of the wind, so serene,
Let nature's embrace remind you of all that you've been.

You are not defined by the battles you endure,
But by the courage within, by the love you secure,
Let these words be a beacon, a lifeline in the fray,
A reminder that there are many who still pray.

Shattered dreams may surround you, like shards on the
floor,
But remember, dear warrior, you are worth fighting for,
With perseverance and love, your spirit shall rise,
Ignite the will to live, to live without compromise.

So, hold on tight, warrior, for your light's indispensable,
A beacon of hope, a strength so commendable,
Fight with every breath, let your battles unfold,
For in this collective journey, love will always enfold.

Shattered Dreams: The Warriors' Call,
Let your anthem resound, standing tall,
Your courage inspires others to follow suit,
To join the battle, to fight and never refute.

Remember, dear warriors, your worth and your might,
Your struggles, your triumphs, your innermost fight,
Though the road may be weary, and the path may seem
long,
You are not alone; in your fight, we all belong.

So, embrace this title, let it shine like a star,
Illuminate the darkness, no matter how far,
Together we stand, united we'll strive,
For the warriors' spirit, forever will thrive.

The Phoenix's Song: Warriors of the Night
by QUEEN ANGELA

In the Darkest Night, the Warrior's Light

Through the abyss, where shadows start to swell,
A battle waged within, a tortured soul,
But hark! Dear warriors, I must bravely tell,
Your strength, your worth, can help make darkness whole.

In solitude you fight, with demons fierce,
Yet in your heart, a fire fiercely burns,
For countless unseen battles you've traversed,
Each scar, a testament, each lesson learned.

Within your veins, a warrior resides,
A flicker of hope, too precious to be lost,
Embrace the strength that in your heart abides,
For victories await, no matter the cost.

So rise, dear warriors, brave and strong,
The world depends on you to right the wrong.

IF YOU NEED HELP CALL 988

A letter to those behind Prison Walls: you are not alone on the journey

Rediscovering Hope and Love: A Message to the Wrongfully Incarcerated Battling Suicidal Thoughts

by QUEEN ANGELA

Dear friend,

To all those who have been wrongfully and overly incarcerated, I cannot even begin to fathom the pain and despair you may be going through. But please, hear my words and let them resonate within you.

Firstly, I want you to know that you are not alone. There are countless others who have faced similar unjust circumstances, and their strength can be a beacon of hope for you. Even in the darkest moments, remember that you are not defined by the mistakes of others, nor by any wrongful convictions.

It is essential to forgive yourself. Recognize that you are a victim of a flawed system, and clinging onto guilt will only further burden your soul. Embrace the power of forgiveness, freeing yourself from the weight of self-blame. Allow this act of forgiveness to be the foundation upon which you rebuild your life.

Understand that there is hope. Your current situation does not dictate your future. While the road to justice may seem long and arduous, do not lose faith. Seek solace in the knowledge that truth and righteousness will prevail.

Hold onto the hope that a brighter and more just future awaits you.

Most importantly, learn to love yourself again. It is easy to fall into a cycle of self-hatred and doubt, but believe me when I say that you are deserving of love and compassion. Treat yourself with kindness and nurture your spirit. Rediscover the inherent worth and dignity that resides within you. Embrace self-love as a catalyst for healing and transformation.

Healing is possible. It may take time, and it may not be easy, but with forgiveness, hope, and self-love, you can begin your journey towards reclaiming your life. Surround yourself with a supportive network of friends, family, or professionals who can guide you along this path.

Remember, you are stronger than you know. You have the power to rise above the pain and darkness. Hold onto forgiveness, hope, and self-love tightly in your heart, for they will be your guides on this journey to healing.

Never lose sight of the fact that you deserve justice, happiness, and a life filled with love. You are not defined by your past but by the strength and resilience that you embody. Together, let us overcome the shadows of injustice and bring light into your life once more.

15

~QUEEN ANGELA ~

POEMS FROM BEHIND THE WALL
WRITTEN BY
ANDREW LEE BEARD

DAILY BATTLES OF A BUTTERFLY
by ALB

The former shade
Accepting light and warmth
To melt the frost of his heart
With trembling wings
Those no longer offend
He is called to help and heal
Stepping in alone
Heart a fire and fluttering
To the cold places of dark and before
No fear of flight
His faith and prayers sustain him

IF YOU NEED HELP CALL 988

Songs of Pensive Shadows Reform
by ALB

So the former shade has procured a faith
Through exquisite trials and countless errors
Now in chaos he patiently waits
Praying the rosary to the sounds of terror
He had found such faith in his youth
Perhaps a choice absent of flesh and violence
Unto a path of absolute truth...
With surety and confidence he prays in silence.

Forgotten Flowers in the Dark
by ALB

Of Shadows and darkness and paths once travled
Unknown to love, or the existence of warmth
A vigilant mind in these cold confines
With naught but will to move through the days
Dreams and hopes of a different world
As enemy's garrison surround that heart
A thousand prayers upon those once prideful lips
For all he is and could have been
The path now taken upon brighter roads
The forgotten flower, in faith has bloomed

IF YOU NEED HELP CALL 988

Rifa Cimento Sanctanimity
by ALB

If you were to make lightning Dance within my heart,
I would Light any other hearts who know only
Darkness. Even if this entire realm Cursed me for my
spark. If you were to sing to me, so that I could recall
love in every form, I would kneel in supplication and
speak my humble petitions with more resolve. Even
if the ground was muddy from these repentant tears I
shed.

17

A QUEEN'S PRAYER

In darkness you find yourself, so alone,
Behind prison walls, your soul silently moans.
But hold on tight, my dear, don't let go,
For there's hope and healing that I know.

In these concrete walls, where dreams seem to fade,
Know that I'm praying, my love, don't be afraid.
A queen's prayers surround you, with every breath,
Sending strength and salvation, conquering death.

Suicide whispers its lies, tries to deceive,
But listen to my voice, believe and receive.
You're not alone, my dear, I promise it's true,
Together we'll conquer, we'll make it through.

Stay encouraged, my warrior, be strong,
You're worth so much, even when things go wrong.
Behind prison walls, remember you are loved,
And your healing, my dear, is not far above.

So hold on tight, keep fighting with all your might,
For I'm praying for you, from morning till night.
Suicide may knock, but it won't break this wall,
For your healing, my dear, is my fervent call.

About the Author

Queen Angela Thomas Smith is a passionate advocate for mental health and wellness, poetry & literacy, and supporting those behind prison walls. With her numerous roles and accomplishments, it's clear that Angela wears many hats and is dedicated to making a positive impact in the world.

As the co-founder of the FREE TEXAS Campaign, Angela is at the forefront of raising awareness to the corruption in the state of TEXAS. She understands that everyone deserves access to the resources and support they need to maintain their mental well-being. Through her work, Angela strives to break down the stigma associated with mental health and ensure that no one suffers in silence.

In addition, Angela is a prolific author, with an impressive 65 books to her name. Her writing reflects her passion for PEOPLE , poetry and literacy, and she uses her words to inspire and uplift others. Whether it's through her poems, magazine or her books, Angela aims to encourage self-reflection, healing, and personal growth.

Furthermore, Angela is a sought-after speaker, coach, podcast host, and magazine owner. Her extensive experience and expertise allow her to deliver impactful presentations, offer valuable coaching sessions, and provide a platform for important conversations through her podcast and magazine. Angela is committed to sharing her knowledge and empowering others to make positive changes in their lives.

With her motto, "We have to be the change we desire to see in this world," Angela exemplifies her dedication to making a difference. She understands that change starts with individual action and believes in the power of collaboration and unity. By working together, Angela believes we can create a world that is more compassionate, understanding, and inclusive.

To connect with Angela or book her for an event, she can be reached at queenofcollaborations@gmail.com. Additionally, you can follow her on linktr.ee/queenofcollaborations to stay updated on her latest projects, writings, and advocacy work.

Overall, Queen Angela Thomas Smith is a remarkable individual who utilizes various platforms and roles to bring awareness to mental health and wellness, promote the power of words through literature and poetry, and support those impacted by the criminal justice system. Her dedication, compassion, and determination serve as an inspiration to others,

9 798210 936073